THE SCIENCE OF THE FUTURE

BEYOND BELIEF

ALEX WOOLF

JASMINE FLOYD

To my amazing children,
Michael and Maya, who fill me
with hope for the future.
- A.W

To my one in a million parents
for always supporting my creative
dreams and giving me the opportunities
you have! I am forever grateful,
this one's for you!
- J.F

The world is an ever-changing place and
the people within it are capable of incredible
things; discoveries are made, records are broken,
new facts are found and history recovered.
We will be happy to revise and update
information in future editions.

360 DEGREES
An imprint of the Little Tiger Group
1 Coda Studios, 189 Munster Road, London SW6 6AW
Imported into the EEA by Penguin Random House Ireland,
Morrison Chambers, 32 Nassau Street, Dublin D02 YH68
www.littletiger.co.uk
First published in Great Britain 2022
Text copyright © 2022 Alex Woolf
Illustrations copyright © 2022 Jasmine Floyd
A CIP catalogue record for this book is
available from the British Library
All rights reserved • Printed in China
ISBN: 978-1-83891-401-1
CPB/2800/2007/1021
2 4 6 8 10 9 7 5 3 1

CONTENTS

INTRODUCTION

We are living in truly exciting times...

Almost every week a technological breakthrough is announced – a new kind of VR headset, a crop-spraying drone or a computer with a flexible screen. Around the world, scientists and engineers are working on revolutionary new inventions that may soon become regular fixtures of our world – driverless cars, intelligent robots, 3D printing and energy from nuclear fusion.

Modern technology develops at a startling pace. People living just thirty years ago might find today's world bewildering, with its smartphones, social media, virtual assistants, video calls and video-sharing websites.

They'd be equally amazed at how these developments have transformed our lives, making us better informed and more connected than ever before.

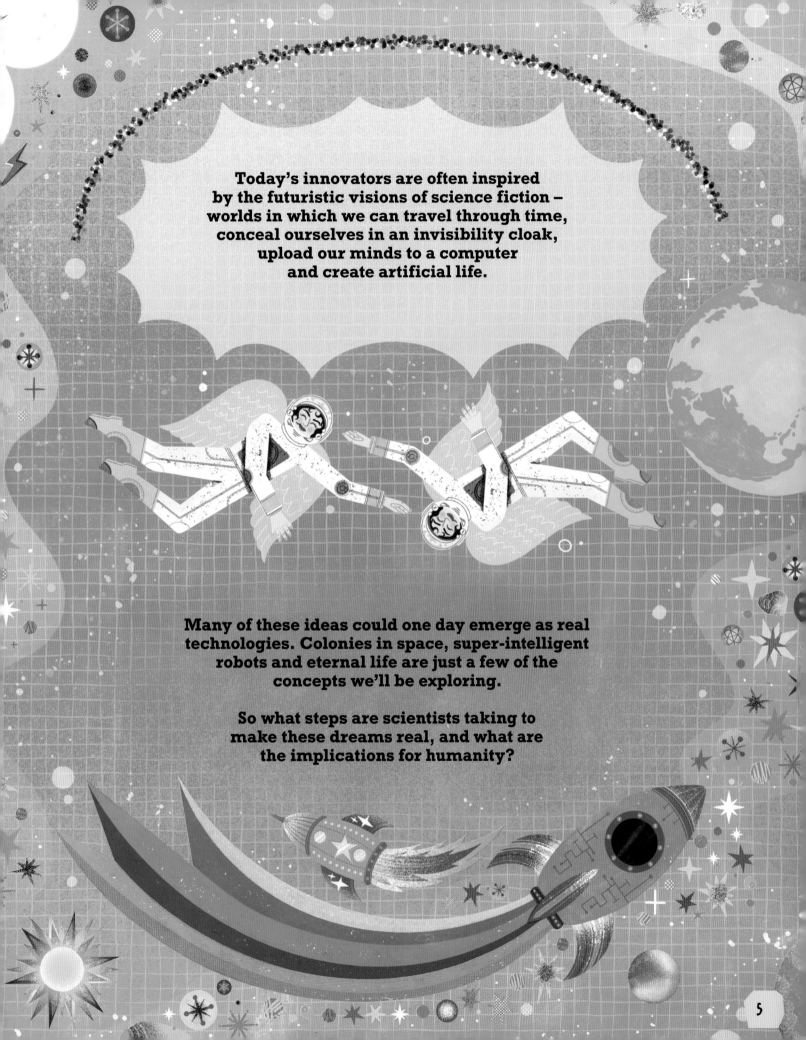

Today's innovators are often inspired
by the futuristic visions of science fiction –
worlds in which we can travel through time,
conceal ourselves in an invisibility cloak,
upload our minds to a computer
and create artificial life.

Many of these ideas could one day emerge as real
technologies. Colonies in space, super-intelligent
robots and eternal life are just a few of the
concepts we'll be exploring.

So what steps are scientists taking to
make these dreams real, and what are
the implications for humanity?

SPACE COLONIES

Today, our survival as a species depends on a single planet. But what if one day something happened to Earth – an asteroid strike, a super-volcano or a climate catastrophe – that threatened human civilisation? We could easily go the way of the dinosaurs...

That's why people have been looking to the stars for our salvation. Could we one day colonise space?

A DANGEROUS PLACE

The problem is, we aren't built to live in space:

✴ There's no air, food or water.

✴ It's a place of extreme temperatures. The Sun-facing side of the International Space Station can reach 121°C (250°F) and the shadow side a freezing -157° C (-250°F).

✴ Lack of gravity is bad for the bones and muscles.

✴ There are high levels of harmful radiation.

Any space colony would have to protect people from these dangers.

If we lived in space for a long time, our bodies would probably adapt, evolving denser bones, for example, to counter the lack of gravity.

Colonists on planets with less sunlight, like Mars, might develop larger eyes to see better.

After thousands of years, colonists might even become a new species.

CASH-TEROIDS?

Asteroids have billions of tonnes of valuable metals, such as iron, nickel, gold and platinum, so colonising space could allow humans to harvest its resources and get rich!

DID YOU KNOW?

One of the earliest stories about building a community in space was *The Brick Moon* by Edward Hale in 1869, about an inhabited artificial satellite.

ANY AIR UP THERE?

The components of air – oxygen, nitrogen and carbon dioxide – can be produced from substances found in space.

Moon rock contains oxygen, which can be harvested using heat and electricity.

Air could be cleaned and recycled for colonists, perhaps by planting a forest in the colony.

SUN POWER

Space colonies would have to be completely self-sufficient. The Sun could provide all the colony's heat and electric power (via solar panels) – although this would decrease the further away from the Sun the colony was.

COSMIC CARROTS

Food, including rice, potatoes and peas, has already been grown on space stations. Nutrients from toilet waste can be used to fertilise crops. In low gravity, roots grow in all directions, and water and nutrients float. Plant seeds need to be glued to little bags filled with soil and fertiliser so the nutrients get to the roots.

COLONIES IN ORBIT

A space colony wouldn't have to be on a planet or moon. It could be based inside an enormous space station orbiting Earth or some other body. The space station would need to rotate to create its own gravity.

In the 1970s, American physicist Gerard O'Neill proposed 'O'Neill Cylinders' – a pair of rotating cylinders, 8km (5mi) wide and 32km (20mi) long, each with an Earthlike interior large enough to support thousands of people.

By contrast, today's International Space Station is 109m (360ft) x 73m (240ft) in size, with a crew of three to six astronauts.

DID YOU KNOW?
An O'Neill Cylinder space colony would be big enough inside for clouds to form.

THE MOON

A future colony on the Moon would be relatively close to Earth, making trade and communications between the two easier.

As the Moon has no atmosphere and harmful radiation, the best location for a colony would be underground, inside a lava tube (a tunnel created by the Moon's ancient rivers of volcanic lava).

Some of these lava tubes are up to 5km (3mi) wide. Water could be obtained from ice at the Moon's poles and used to generate oxygen through a process called electrolysis.

EUROPA AND TITAN

Saturn's biggest moon, Titan, has an atmosphere containing oxygen, hydrogen, nitrogen and methane – all elements necessary for life – making it perhaps the most hospitable world in our solar system for human colonisation.

EUROPA

DID YOU KNOW?

On Titan, gravity is so low and the atmosphere is so dense, a human could strap on a pair of wings and fly.

TITAN

Scientists believe that Jupiter's fourth biggest moon, Europa, has an ocean beneath its icy surface, which may even contain life.

This might be the only possible location on Europa for a human colony as the moon's surface is extremely cold, with high levels of radiation.

MARS

Mars has no atmosphere, so colonists would have to live inside artificial habitats with their own life-support systems.

Frequent dust storms may require satellites to beam solar energy wirelessly to the Martian surface.

Caves near the volcano Arsia Mons or lava tubes might be good sites for a base.

Some scientists believe Mars could be 'terraformed' by gradually changing its atmosphere and climate to make it hospitable to human life.

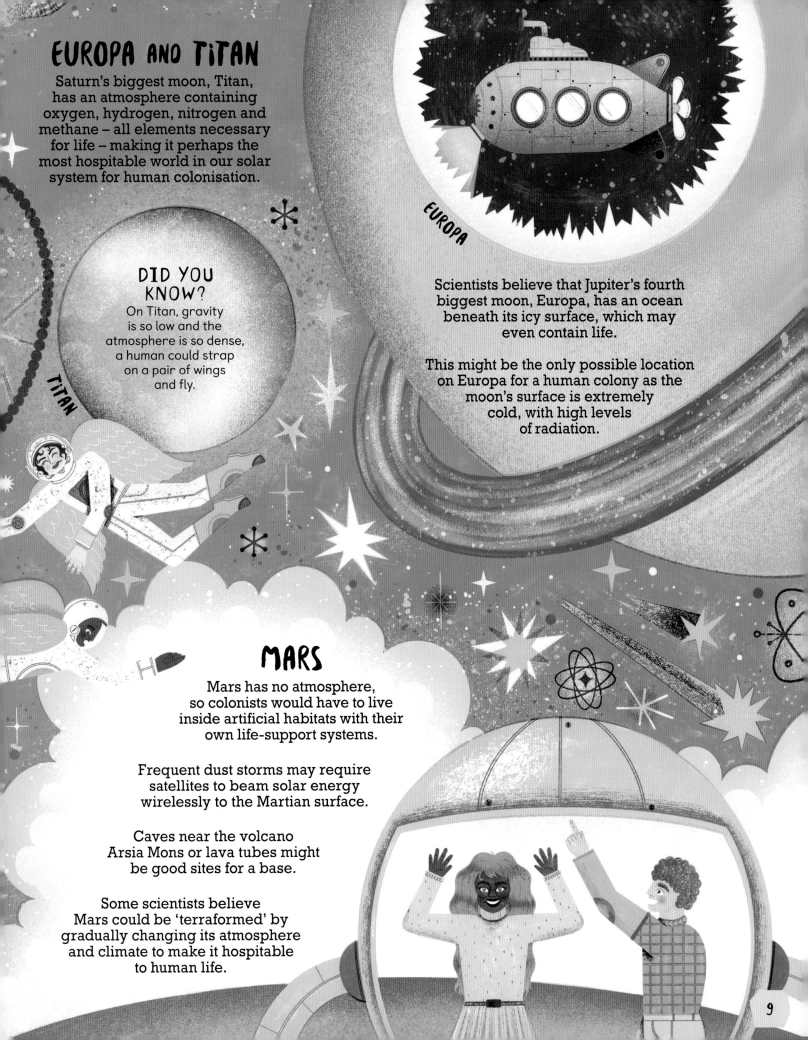

SUPER-INTELLIGENT MACHINES

COMPOSE MUSIC

PLAY CHESS

DIAGNOSE DISEASE

Perhaps the most popular character in all of science fiction is the intelligent robot. Audiences are happy to accept thinking, feeling movie robots, but will it ever be possible to build a machine with humanlike intelligence?

Until recently, this idea seemed like a fantasy. But huge progress in artificial intelligence (AI) has meant that, today, AI programmes are used to diagnose diseases, compose music, translate languages and recognise faces.

In some ways, AI programmes are far more advanced than humans. They can perform millions of calculations a second and can beat humans at games such as chess.

Yet we shouldn't get too excited. So far, no machine has ever fallen in love, or appreciated a beautiful sunset. Machines don't know that they exist. In other words, they aren't conscious like humans.

PEPPER

TRANSLATE LANGUAGES

Hello 你好

ROBOT BUDDIES

Robots' lack of consciousness hasn't stopped them being used as companions. 'Pepper', released in 2015, is programmed to recognise faces, read basic human emotions and talk to its human friends.

Humans are naturally sociable and can often feel lonely, so it's very likely that robots will continue to be used in this way to provide friendship.

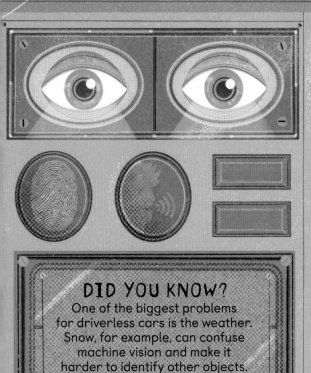

COMPUTER-CONTROLLED CARS

Sometimes, it's their very lack of humanity that makes machines useful to us. They don't get angry, tired or lose concentration, making them ideal drivers. Driverless vehicles are linked to AI programmes that can see, hear, think and make decisions.

In the future, driverless cars will be connected to the road network and traffic signals, as well as each other, enabling them to decide on the best and safest routes.

DID YOU KNOW?
One of the biggest problems for driverless cars is the weather. Snow, for example, can confuse machine vision and make it harder to identify other objects.

CAN COMPUTERS SEE?

Machines can be brilliant in some areas and struggle in others. Most people find it easy to identify an apple in a tree or read an angry expression because humans have spent millions of years using their eyes to find food and evade danger. However, computers can have trouble working out where an object ends and a background begins.

COMPUTER EYE

HUMAN EYE

Yet, thanks to their increasing power and ability to learn from their mistakes, computers are getting much better at analysing visual data. This allows them to do things humans can't, such as reconstruct a scene from different angles, restore damaged or blurry images and estimate the speed of an object in a video.

CAN MACHINES THINK AND FEEL?

So computers can display friendship, drive cars and recognise objects. But will they ever become truly conscious? Could a self-driving car one day decide to deviate from its programmed route and go its own way?

Some scientists believe that consciousness isn't necessarily unique to humans. It happens because our brains work in a certain way, and there's nothing to stop it from happening in an artificial brain too.

The problem is we don't yet know how human consciousness happens. Once we've cracked that, machine consciousness might be just a short step away.

But even if machine consciousness isn't possible, as long as they *appear* conscious to us – by laughing at our jokes or telling us about their 'thoughts' and 'memories' – it'll be much like talking to a person...

SUPER AI

What does seem likely is machine super-intelligence – the emergence of machines that are far superior to even the brightest humans.

These machines would have perfect memories, an internet-sized brain and be able to do hundreds of activities at once.

They could even connect with each other to create one all-knowing super-mind. A machine with intelligence on this scale could pose a threat to the human race.

13

A ROBOT REVOLUTION

Already, robots and AI systems are replacing humans in all sorts of jobs, including manual labour, translation, legal and financial research and even some kinds of journalism.

But could a super-intelligent machine one day take over the world? It's possible – once it can outthink us and take actions we can't foresee or guard against.

If a super-machine decided that humans posed a risk to itself or to its resources, it may even decide to dispose of us...

CATASTRO-PHONE

It's possible that an AI takeover could happen by accident. If a machine was programmed to, say, make as many smartphones as possible, it might decide to take over the planet so that it could use all its resources to make phones.

It could decide to kill or imprison all humans to stop them shutting it down, or use the Earth's resources to make different things.

As machines get smarter, it becomes ever more important for us to embed safeguards in their programming so they don't end up harming us.

HOW COULD IT HAPPEN?

Why not just unplug the machine before it takes over? An artificial super-intelligence could get around this by spreading itself through our computer systems like a virus.

14

TIME TRAVEL

We are all time travellers, heading into the future at a rate of exactly one hour per hour. It doesn't feel like time travel because we're doing it together. Usually by time travel, we mean someone's personal time getting out of step with this process.

So, if we travelled faster than one hour per hour, we'd reach the future before anyone else; travelling slower than that speed would take us to the past.

PAST AND FUTURE

So, do the past and future actually exist, and are they places we could visit? We know from photos and our memories that the past exists.

As for the future, scientists disagree on whether it's fixed like the past or constantly being formed due to our actions.

If it's fluid, then what would we be visiting? Just one of many possible futures? If it's fixed, we'd have no power to change it.

TIME TRICKERY

If you went back in time, you could prevent your mother and father from meeting, meaning that you were never born. But if you were never born, who went back in time to prevent them from meeting? This is called a paradox – an absurd or contradictory idea.

2020

2040

FAST TO THE FUTURE

In the early 20th century, German physicist Albert Einstein demonstrated the possibility of time travel to the future by showing that the speed of light (roughly 300,000km [186,000mi] per second) is the top speed limit of the universe, and the closer we get to that speed, the more time slows down for us. This is called 'time dilation'.

Because of time dilation, if you travel close to the speed of light in a spacecraft, you'll find on your return to Earth that everyone else is a good deal older. In other words, you've travelled to their future!

DID YOU KNOW?

Einstein's theory of time dilation was proved by experiment in 1971. Scientists placed a highly accurate atomic clock on a commercial jet, where time moved very slightly more slowly than on the ground.

When the plane flew westwards, clocks gained 179 billionths of a second – in line with Einstein's predictions. So every time you fly in a plane, you're travelling a tiny bit into the future of those on Earth's surface!

GRAVITY TIME

Time doesn't only slow down for speedy travellers; it also moves more slowly for people living on large bodies, such as Earth. This is because gravity warps time.

At the moment, we lack the technology to travel anywhere near the speed of light, and the amount of energy required would be enormous. Also, as a spacecraft gets close to light speed, it is likely to experience a huge amount of drag.

PATH TO THE PAST

Einstein understood that space and time are linked in a single system called 'space-time'. He envisaged folding space-time, with the help of a powerful gravitational field, to create a short-cut between two locations. We call this short-cut a wormhole. It could take you to another place in space and time, including somewhere in the past.

HOW iT WORKS

How is time linked to space? We're constantly moving through time as well as space, even when we're sitting still. Looked at in this way, time is just the fourth dimension of space (after length, depth and height).

The reason time feels different to the other dimensions is that we're three-dimensional beings. A four-dimensional being would be able to travel along the time dimension, visiting the future and the past as easily as we move through space.

WOBBLY WORMHOLES

A wormhole is like a tunnel with two openings, each emerging at a different point in space-time. Einstein's theories allow for the existence of wormholes, but do they exist in reality? Scientists are searching for evidence. Even if they find them, wormholes are likely to be very unstable and prone to collapse.

HOW IT WORKS

Imagine space-time as a piece of paper and you want to get from near the top to near the bottom. If you fold the paper in two, you could punch a hole through it, connecting the start and end points of your journey and making it quicker. That's how to imagine a wormhole.

DARK ENERGY

In the 1990s, astronomers discovered that the expansion of the universe was speeding up. This may be due to a mysterious anti-gravity force they call 'dark energy', which is pushing everything apart. This dark energy could be used to traverse the wormhole.

It may be possible to build a time machine by grabbing and manipulating a wormhole. Its mouth would need to be held open somehow to allow a traveller to pass through it. Scientists think this could be done using dark energy.

BUILDING A TIME MACHINE

American physicist Ron Mallett suggested a time machine could be built using a laser to produce a circular beam of light. If powerful enough, the space inside this 'ring laser' would become warped, like coffee being stirred by a spoon.

Warping space like this would also warp time, because the two are linked. If time was twisted into a loop, Mallett believes that would allow the possibility of travelling to the past.

TIME MACHINE

NORMAL PASSAGE OF TIME

FUTURE

PAST

DID YOU KNOW?

On 28 June 2009, Stephen Hawking threw a 'time travellers' party'. Invitations were sent out only after the party was over.

Not surprisingly, no one showed up. If they had, it would have proved Hawking wrong in his theory that time travel to the past is impossible.

PROTECTING THE PAST

Some scientists believe that time travellers to the past wouldn't be able to change anything – something would happen to prevent them causing all sorts of paradoxes (see p.15). British physicist Stephen Hawking's 'chronology protection conjecture' suggested that a time-machine wormhole would probably explode if anyone tried to use it.

INVISIBILITY

Since ancient times, people have dreamed
of having the power to make themselves invisible.
In myths and legends, characters sometimes wear an
invisibility cap, cloak, ring or amulet in order to act
secretly or avoid detection by their enemies.

But could scientists one day develop a
real-life invisibility device? The key problem
is that light bounces off most physical objects back
to our eyes, and that's how we see them. So, to make
an object invisible, you must find a way of making
light pass through or around it without
reflecting off it.

DID YOU KNOW?

Optical camouflage is an invisibility
technique borrowed from Hollywood filmmakers.
It's a complex process involving a camera, a computer,
a special mirror and a highly reflective garment.
Essentially, you film what's behind you and
project it onto the front of your body,
making you appear invisible.

BENDING LIGHT

One promising development involves
metamaterials. These are artificial materials with
a special kind of light-bending lattice structure. If constructed
in the right way, the metamaterial will guide the light around
an object, much like a boulder diverting water in a stream.

So far, the technology only works
for tiny two-dimensional objects just
ten millionths of a metre in size.

SPECTRAL CLOAKING

In 2018, researchers in Canada managed to make an object invisible using a new technique they call 'spectral cloaking'.

They shone a laser light at an object covered with the cloaking device. The device changed the frequency of the light so it passed right through the object rather than reflecting off it. Once it was beyond the object, the device returned the light to its original frequency.

DID YOU KNOW?

Many objects we make are already invisible – just not to light waves. For example, stealth aircraft are invisible to radio waves and are therefore able to avoid radar detection.

Similarly, soldiers can wear special cloaks to shield them from thermal imaging cameras.

MIRAGE EFFECT

When driving on hot days, you sometimes see what looks like a puddle of water on the road ahead. This mirage occurs because of the temperature difference between the road and the air above it, which causes the light rays to bend so that a patch of sky is visible on the ground. Scientists have found a way of using this effect to create an invisibility device.

A sheet of carbon nanotubes (rolled-up sheets of carbon just one atom thick) is heated up, and the heat is transferred to a surrounding dish of water. Light bends away from the sheet, turning what's behind it invisible.

The object would need to be tiny and immersed in water, so this isn't exactly the most practical of invisibility cloaks!

21

In Greek mythology, Prince Lynceus had the power
to see through solid surfaces. This helped him to find buried
gold and to detect enemies. Comic book hero Superman also possesses
this ability, though it can be thwarted by certain materials such as lead.

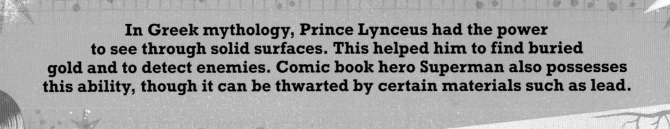

X-RAY VISION

In reality, we already have devices that can see
beneath solid surfaces – X-ray machines. They're used
by doctors to look inside the body, and in airports to check
luggage. But wouldn't it be cool to have this ability ourselves?
We'd probably want to be able to switch it on and off though –
or else we'd live in a world of skeletons!

HOW IT WORKS

X-rays are like visible light, but with much shorter
wavelengths. This allows them to pass through certain
substances, such as human flesh, while getting blocked
by denser substances, such as bone.

To an X-ray machine, human flesh and organs are
virtually transparent, while bones show up
as shadows on the film, creating an X-ray image.

TURNING THE WORLD TRANSPARENT

Superman never reveals how his special power works – perhaps he can beam X-rays from his eyes, and when they hit a bone, for example, they bounce back to his eyes just as light does to normal eyes.

However, X-rays don't bounce back. They are absorbed by bone and other dense substances. Sadly, it seems that Superman's X-ray vision is beyond the reach of science.

WI-FI EYES

If we can't have X-ray vision, perhaps 'radio vision' is possible with a new technology that can sense people on the other side of a wall.

The device sends radio waves in the form of Wi-Fi signals through a wall, which bounce off the body and back to a sensor.

The device can create a detailed image of a person, track their movements and even identify them.

It does this by detecting subtle movements and using AI to fill in the blanks. It could be used by firefighters searching for survivors in a burning house and police staking out suspects.

DID YOU KNOW?

Natalya Demkina is a Russian woman who claims she can look inside human bodies, see organs and tissues and diagnose diseases. She calls this 'medical vision'.

Despite many stories of her successful diagnoses, the scientific community remain unconvinced by her claims.

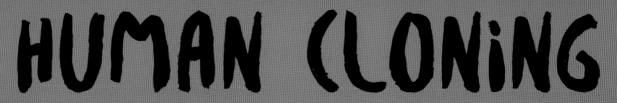

HUMAN CLONING

A clone is a genetically identical copy of an animal or plant. Identical twins are clones – both came from the same fertilised egg. This doesn't mean they're totally identical – they will have different fingerprints and may have different heights and weights.

Our genes play a key role in determining how we look and some aspects of our character, but we are also influenced by our individual experiences.

DNA

CREATURE CLONES

In the 20th century, scientists found a way to create clones artificially, and in 1962 they cloned a frog. The first successfully cloned mammal was Dolly the sheep in 1995.

Since then, many other mammals have been cloned, but what's stopping scientists from creating the first human clone?

WHAT IS IT?

A gene is the part of an organism that determines how it looks and behaves. Your genes came from your parents.

They are carried inside threadlike structures called chromosomes in the nucleus of every cell in your body. Chromosomes are made of long, twisted strands of a molecule called DNA.

PERILOUS PROCESS

Technically, there's nothing to stop us from trying to clone a human, but there are moral issues to consider. It's a risky process. For every successful clone, there are many that die before birth. Some are born with fatal defects. The technology has become safer in recent years, but it is not yet reliable.

HOW IT WORKS

DONOR OF EGG CELL

1. First remove an egg cell from an adult of a particular species.

EGG WITH NUCLEUS REMOVED

2. Take out its nucleus (this contains the genes).

3. Implant this in an egg cell that has had its nucleus removed.

NUCLEUS

EMBRYO

4. Give the egg a tiny electric shock to initiate growth.

5. Once the embryo is growing normally, implant it into the womb of a mother of the same species.

SURROGATE MOTHER

CLONE

CLONING KIDNEYS?

Some believe human cloning could be used in future to help patients who need organ transplants. Cells taken from the patient (the host) would be used to clone an embryo (unborn child). Special cells called stem cells would be taken from the embryo and used to generate the new organ.

This organ would be genetically identical to the host, so the body would not reject it. But this process would destroy the embryo and many people believe we have no right to do this, even if it saves the life of the host.

Nuclear fusion may well be the future of energy for our planet. It powers the Sun and stars, and scientists believe that if they can recreate it on Earth, it could provide us with an almost limitless and pollution-free source of energy. The technology has yet to be made affordable and practical for mass production.

NUCLEAR

ENERGY

PLASMA

FORCING ATOMS TOGETHER

Nuclear fusion joins two lighter elements to form a heavier one (so two hydrogen atoms can fuse to form one helium atom). This releases lots of energy.

Fusing two atoms of any element is tricky because the nucleus of an atom contains protons (positively charged particles), and particles with the same charge repel each other, like magnets.

FUSION

HEAT AND PRESSURE

Nuclear fusion requires two main conditions: extreme heat and pressure. Very high temperatures (hundreds of millions of degrees Celsius) will strip atoms of their electrons (negatively charged particles) to create a gas called plasma. Extreme pressures then squeeze the nucleii of the atoms together.

These conditions, which exist at the Sun's core, are reproduced in fusion reactors. Powerful magnets heat and squeeze gases until they form plasma. The magnets hold the plasma in place so it can't touch the sides of the reactor chamber as it's far too hot for any solid material to withstand.

DID YOU KNOW?

NASA is hoping to develop small-scale nuclear fusion reactors to power its rockets. The reactor would be fuelled by hydrogen, found in the atmosphere of many planets, so the rocket could refuel en route.

The enormous thrust generated by a fusion-powered rocket could cut journey times to Mars from seven to three months and allow a return trip to Jupiter in just two years.

BIG BENEFITS

Nuclear fusion has many advantages over other fuels.

✸ It's abundant: it requires two forms of hydrogen – deuterium, which can be extracted from seawater; and tritium, which can be extracted from the common element lithium.

✸ It's safe: unlike nuclear energy, it doesn't produce radiation or dangerous nuclear waste.

✸ It's clean: unlike fossil fuels, such as coal and oil, it doesn't produce air pollution.

DID YOU KNOW?

The International Thermonuclear Experimental Reactor (ITER), a nuclear fusion reactor in southern France, will feature the world's biggest superconducting magnets. Its powerful magnetic field will contain a plasma around ten times hotter than the core of the Sun.

FASTER-THAN-LIGHT TRAVEL

Light travels at 299,792km (186,282mi) per second. According to the known laws of physics, it's the fastest speed anything can travel. That's because any object with mass requires energy to accelerate, and accelerating an object past the speed of light would take an infinite amount of energy.

This may prove a problem if we ever want to explore the galaxy. Our nearest star, apart from the Sun, is Proxima Centauri, which is 4.24 light years away. That means it takes the light of that star, travelling at the speed of light, 4.24 years to reach Earth.

A spacecraft travelling at a maximum of 56,000kmph (34,800mph) (the top speed of the NASA spacecraft Deep Space 1) would take over 81,000 years to reach Proxima Centauri. That's more than 2,700 human generations!

The galaxy is vast, and to explore it in a reasonable timeframe, we'd need to find a way of travelling quicker than light. Will that ever be possible?

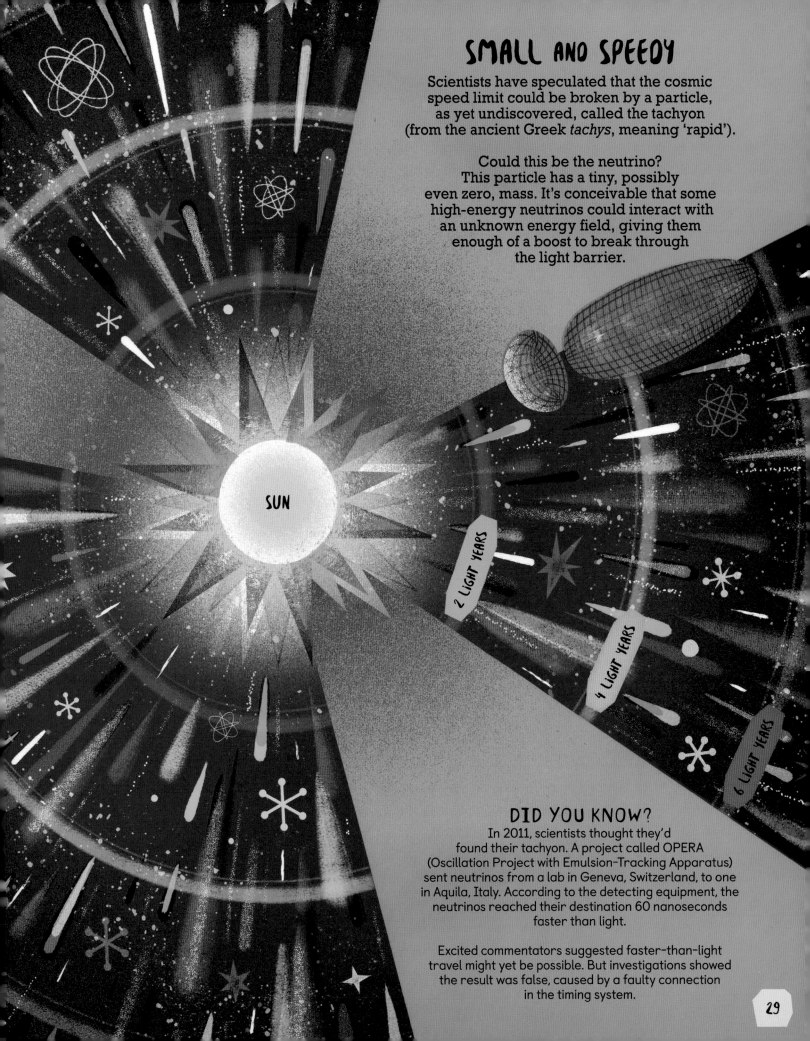

SMALL AND SPEEDY

Scientists have speculated that the cosmic speed limit could be broken by a particle, as yet undiscovered, called the tachyon (from the ancient Greek *tachys*, meaning 'rapid').

Could this be the neutrino? This particle has a tiny, possibly even zero, mass. It's conceivable that some high-energy neutrinos could interact with an unknown energy field, giving them enough of a boost to break through the light barrier.

SUN

2 LIGHT YEARS

4 LIGHT YEARS

6 LIGHT YEARS

DID YOU KNOW?

In 2011, scientists thought they'd found their tachyon. A project called OPERA (Oscillation Project with Emulsion-Tracking Apparatus) sent neutrinos from a lab in Geneva, Switzerland, to one in Aquila, Italy. According to the detecting equipment, the neutrinos reached their destination 60 nanoseconds faster than light.

Excited commentators suggested faster-than-light travel might yet be possible. But investigations showed the result was false, caused by a faulty connection in the timing system.

VR HEADSETS: A WORLD IN YOUR HEAD

Today's VR (virtual reality) headsets provide an immersive, computer-generated environment. They track head and eye movements, giving the illusion of a world all around us.

The headsets can struggle with resolution (the degree of visible detail), colour and distortion and can make users feel sick. But these are technical issues that will one day almost certainly be fixed.

HOW IT WORKS

The VR headset can display images at around 60 frames per second (anything over 12 FPS we perceive as motion). It tracks our eye and head movements using devices that measure our acceleration, degree of tilt and position relative to Earth's magnetic field. The headset's computer absorbs this data and shifts the picture as the user looks around.

IMMERSIVE VIRTUAL REALITY

Some scientists have suggested that our entire world could be fake, and we're all just characters living in a giant computer simulation. This disturbing idea is surprisingly hard to disprove.

We could test the theory by creating a realistic artificial world ourselves – an 'immersive virtual reality'. Could we create something that's indistinguishable from the real world – assuming our own world is real, of course?

GLOVES, SUITS AND TREADMILLS

VR users can also wear data gloves and even full-body suits to interact with the virtual environment. This 'haptic technology' gives us the sense we're touching something solid. Multi-directional treadmills let us move through the alternate world.

One day, no doubt, there will be ways of adding in the sensations of taste and smell to complete our immersion in this unreal world.

STRAIGHT TO THE BRAIN

The ultimate in immersive virtual reality would be to dispense with headsets, gloves and suits and feed these perceptions directly into our brains.

Whether this is possible or even desirable remains to be seen. We might end up permanently inside a giant computer simulation – as some people fear we already are!

sensorama

DID YOU KNOW?

In 1962, filmmaker Morton Heilig developed a machine called the Sensorama. Users could experience riding a motorcycle through New York City.

They saw a 3D street view, felt the wind and the vibration of the motorcycle and could even smell the city air. It was the first attempt at immersive virtual reality.

iMMORTALiTY

Throughout history, humans have feared and wished to conquer death. One of the earliest works of literature, *The Epic of Gilgamesh*, written 2,400 years ago, is about a hero's quest for immortality.

In ancient China, alchemists spent centuries trying to develop an elixir of eternal life. One such attempt led to the accidental invention of gunpowder.

DID YOU KNOW?

In the Vedic hymns of ancient India, *amrita* and *soma* are names given to the legendary drink of immortality.

The ancient Greeks referred to it as *ambrosia*, or *nektar* – which means 'overcoming death'.

In medieval Europe, the fabled philosopher's stone was said to grant unending life.

122

LiVING LONGER

These days we turn to science, technology and medicine in our quest for immortality. The average human lifespan has rocketed over the last century.

In 1900, average life expectancy was 47 years. By 2016, it was 72 years. As of 2021, the record for the longest life is held by Jeanne Calment of France, who died aged 122 in 1997.

So, is there an upper limit to the human lifespan, or could we actually achieve immortality?

WHAT DO WE MEAN BY iMMORTALiTY?

122

If we mean 'indestructibility', like a comic book superhero, then the answer is probably no – we could be run over by a bus. As for getting older and frailer but never dying, who would want that? What most people mean by immortality is remaining eternally young, at one's peak of mental and physical strength.

HOW DOES IT WORK?

In order to understand whether it's possible to stop the ageing process, we first have to look at what causes the body to age. Scientists have found three key causes of ageing. These are:

GLYCATION

A process whereby sugar molecules attach themselves to protein and fat molecules in the body, leading to a loss in skin elasticity, the formation of wrinkles and free radicals.

OXIDATIVE STRESS

This is caused when our bodies contain too many free radicals (unstable molecules we take in when we breathe). Oxidative stress is a natural process, but over time it leads to cell and tissue damage.

TELOMERE SHORTENING

Chromosomes are the threadlike structures in our cells that carry our genes. Telomeres, like plastic tips on a shoelace, prevent chromosomes from fraying. But telomeres get shorter each time a cell divides. This limits cells' ability to keep dividing, leading to ageing.

If these processes can be greatly reduced or stopped altogether, immortality may be within our reach.

THE 'DRACULA' METHOD

Scientists have noticed that the GDF11 protein is very common in the blood of young mice but is rare in older mice. This protein, also found in humans, increases skeletal muscle and heart strength.

Regular transfusions of young blood could perhaps extend our lifespans by up to 20 years. This 'vampire-like' behaviour may become normal practice in the next few decades.

DID YOU KNOW?

Drug companies are trying to develop pills that stop us ageing. One pill destroys the old cells that stay in the body causing ill health. Another contains a chemical that helps cells release energy from glucose – supplementing a natural substance within us that declines with age.

LONG-LIFE GENE

Are our genes responsible for how long we live? As we grow older, our DNA (the molecule that carries genetic information) is prone to breaks, leading to cancer and ageing. The DNA repairs itself, but less efficiently in mammals with shorter lifespans.

In 2019, researchers at the University of Rochester in New York, USA, discovered that a gene, sirtuin 6, ensures more efficient DNA repair in species with longer lifespans.

The human form of sirtuin 6 is already very efficient, but it may be that mammals like the bowhead whale, which lives more than 200 years, have evolved an even stronger version of this gene. Could this be the secret to a longer life?

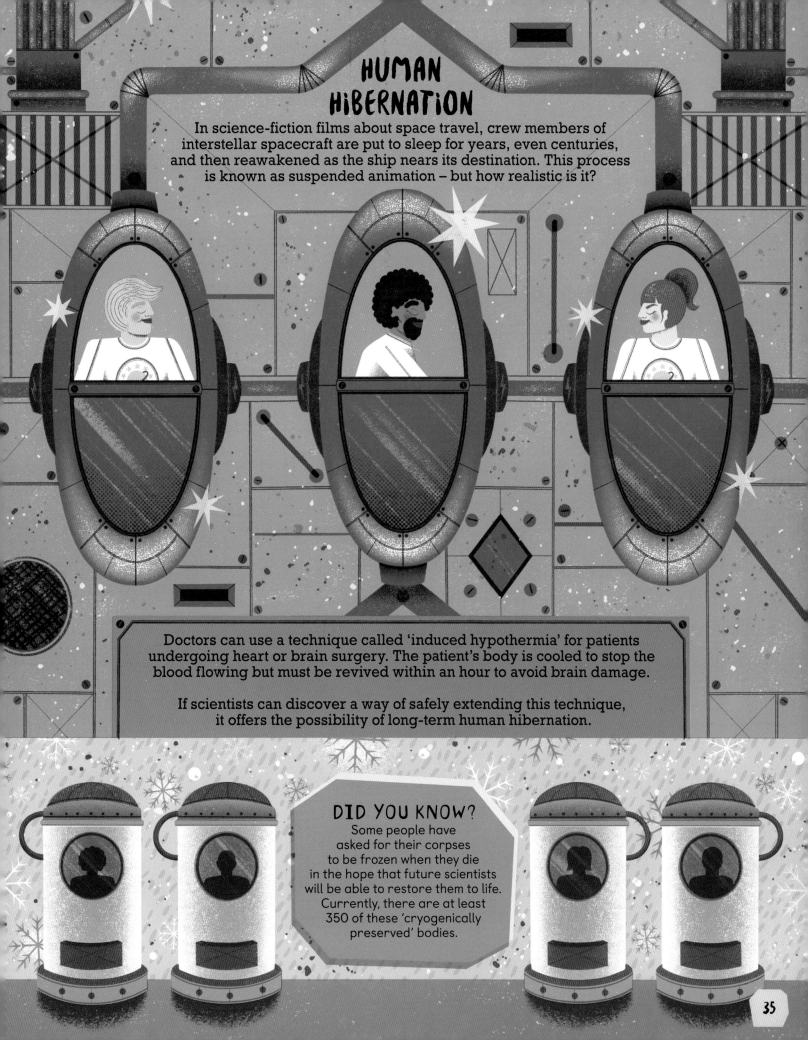

HUMAN HIBERNATION

In science-fiction films about space travel, crew members of interstellar spacecraft are put to sleep for years, even centuries, and then reawakened as the ship nears its destination. This process is known as suspended animation – but how realistic is it?

Doctors can use a technique called 'induced hypothermia' for patients undergoing heart or brain surgery. The patient's body is cooled to stop the blood flowing but must be revived within an hour to avoid brain damage.

If scientists can discover a way of safely extending this technique, it offers the possibility of long-term human hibernation.

DID YOU KNOW?
Some people have asked for their corpses to be frozen when they die in the hope that future scientists will be able to restore them to life. Currently, there are at least 350 of these 'cryogenically preserved' bodies.

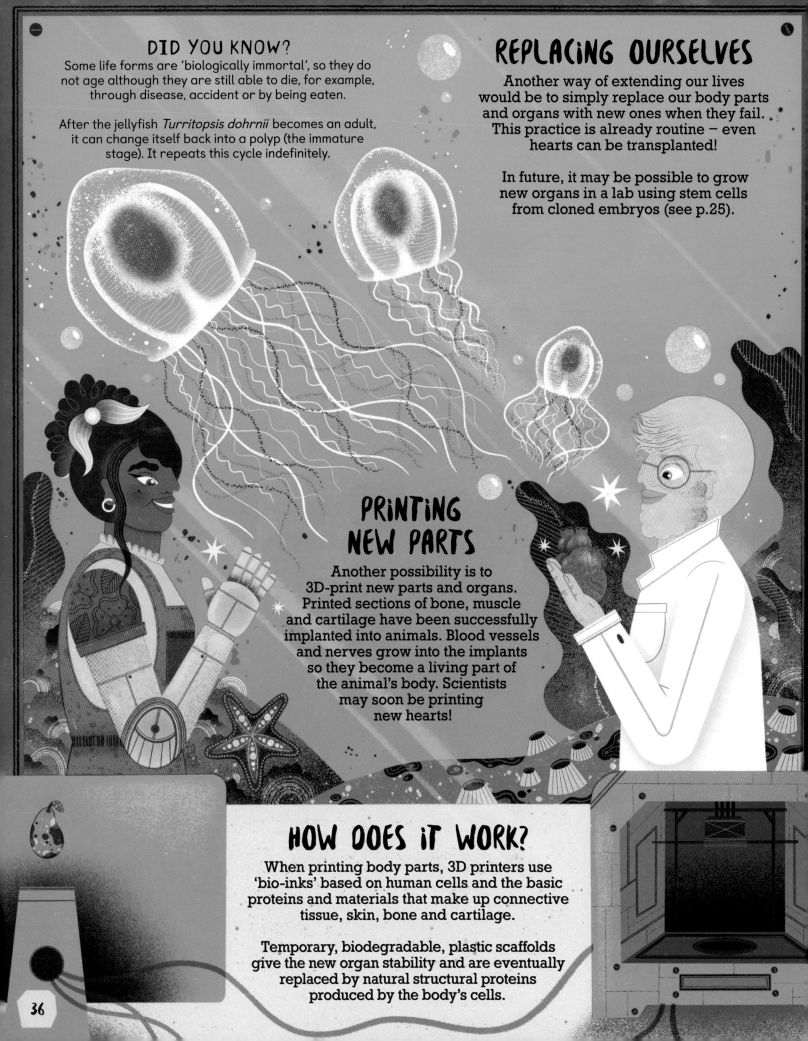

DID YOU KNOW?

Some life forms are 'biologically immortal', so they do not age although they are still able to die, for example, through disease, accident or by being eaten.

After the jellyfish *Turritopsis dohrnii* becomes an adult, it can change itself back into a polyp (the immature stage). It repeats this cycle indefinitely.

REPLACING OURSELVES

Another way of extending our lives would be to simply replace our body parts and organs with new ones when they fail. This practice is already routine – even hearts can be transplanted!

In future, it may be possible to grow new organs in a lab using stem cells from cloned embryos (see p.25).

PRINTING NEW PARTS

Another possibility is to 3D-print new parts and organs. Printed sections of bone, muscle and cartilage have been successfully implanted into animals. Blood vessels and nerves grow into the implants so they become a living part of the animal's body. Scientists may soon be printing new hearts!

HOW DOES IT WORK?

When printing body parts, 3D printers use 'bio-inks' based on human cells and the basic proteins and materials that make up connective tissue, skin, bone and cartilage.

Temporary, biodegradable, plastic scaffolds give the new organ stability and are eventually replaced by natural structural proteins produced by the body's cells.

IS IMMORTALITY SUCH A GOOD IDEA?

Many of us are attracted to the idea of extending our lifespan, or even living forever. As technological advances bring us closer to this goal, we should ask ourselves what the impact of immortality would be.

If people stopped dying, the population would skyrocket. Would the world have the resources to feed all of us immortals?

What if the life-extending treatments could only be afforded by the super-rich? We might soon find ourselves in a very unequal society, divided between an immortal elite and everyone else.

What would it feel like to be immortal? It might be wonderful at first – all that time to read, travel and learn new skills. But after several centuries, you might feel that you'd done everything worth doing and start to get bored…

TELEPORTATION

Imagine being able to travel anywhere in an instant without needing to physically cross the space in between. No more traffic jams, no more flight delays. Interplanetary travel could be yours at the flick of a switch. That is the promise of teleportation.

HOW DOES IT WORK?

The theory behind teleportation is that your body could be scanned, atom by atom, and this data would then be beamed to a computer, which would reassemble a perfect copy of you at your desired destination.

SPOOKY ACTION AT A DISTANCE

In 1993, a team of scientists showed how it would be possible, in principle, to teleport a photon (a light particle). The scientists pointed to a phenomenon called 'quantum entanglement' in which a pair of particles affect each other, even when separated by vast distances.

If you change the state of one particle, the state of the other particle changes too. Einstein called it 'spooky action at a distance'. The scientists said it should be possible to use a pair of entangled particles to send information about a third particle.

WHAT IS IT?

A quantum is a discrete unit, or packet, of energy.

A quantum of light, for example, is called a photon.

bread
milk

SUCCESS

In 1998, physicists at the California Institute of Technology, USA, used quantum entanglement to teleport a photon across 1m (3ft) of cable. They scanned the photon, beamed the data and created a replica at the other end. As predicted, the original photon was destroyed in the process.

Since then, further advances have been made. In 2002, an Australian team teleported a laser beam. In 2012, researchers in China teleported a photon 97km (60mi), and in 2017 another Chinese team was able to teleport photons to a satellite 1,400km (870mi) away.

IT MIGHT BE QUICKER TO WALK

Teleporting photons is one thing; it's another matter entirely to teleport a human being. Assuming we manage to advance to teleporting atoms in the next decade, humans are made up of more than a trillion trillion atoms. In terms of data, that's a lot of bits (2.6 followed by 42 zeroes!). It would take much longer to transfer that amount of data than the time the universe has existed.

NANOTECHNOLOGY

There's a whole universe at the tips of your fingers – literally!
This is the universe at the nanoscale – the scale of atoms
and molecules. In recent decades, scientists have
started to penetrate the nanoscale.

Like explorers of an alien planet, they have found
a world quite unlike our own, where materials
behave in different and unexpected ways.

There are applications in medicine,
computing, materials science,
food, energy production
and many other areas.

This is nanotechnology –
and it has the potential
to revolutionise
our world.

HOW SMALL ARE WE TALKING?

At the nanoscale, things are measured
in nanometres, which is a billionth of a metre.
To get a picture of how tiny this is, a sheet of newspaper
is 100,000 nanometres thick, and a bacterium is 200 nanometres
long. An atom is between 0.1 and 0.5 of a nanometre in diameter.

WELCOME TO THE NANOVERSE

At the nanoscale, the laws of physics work differently. Gravity is much less important than the electromagnetic forces that operate between atoms and molecules. This can give substances different properties: copper becomes transparent; carbon becomes very hard. Extremely thin materials, such as graphene, can be made in sheets just one atom thick.

Nanoparticles are bumpy, which gives them a greater surface area and means they tend to be more chemically reactive. Gold is non-reactive at our scale but reacts readily with other substances at the nanoscale. Size also affects a substance's strength and conductivity.

DID YOU KNOW?

On 29 December 1959, American physicist Richard Feynman gave a talk entitled 'There's Plenty of Room at the Bottom'. He suggested that scientists could one day use tiny tools to rearrange atoms and molecules. This ignited interest in the idea of nanotechnology.

HOW TO SEE ATOMS

Atoms can't be seen through an ordinary microscope. To see an object, it must deflect visible light waves, and an atom is much smaller than the wavelength of visible light.

So, scientists have developed electron microscopes. These use electron beams that have wavelengths thousands of times shorter than light beams.

Electron wavelengths are so short they are deflected by atoms and can therefore generate images at this scale. Electron microscopes can magnify images by more than a million times.

Some show the atomic structure inside materials; others show the atoms and molecules on the surface.

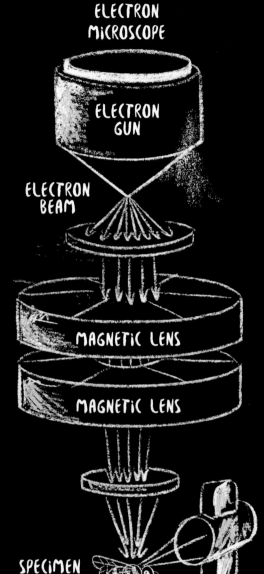

ELECTRON MICROSCOPE

ELECTRON GUN

ELECTRON BEAM

MAGNETIC LENS

MAGNETIC LENS

ELECTRON DETECTOR

SPECIMEN

HOW DOES IT WORK?

To use an electron microscope, the specimen being examined is first placed inside a vacuum (airless chamber) because electrons travel better in a vacuum.

Then a beam of electrons is fired at the specimen from a gun at the top of the chamber.

The beam passes through a series of coil-shaped electromagnets that hugely accelerate the electrons – the faster they travel, the smaller the waves they form and the more detailed the image.

The beam passes through the specimen before striking a photographic plate to create an image.

DID YOU KNOW?

Fingernails grow at one nanometre per second.

Nanotubes have been used to create bullet-proof business suits.

In 1989, IBM engineer Don Eigler became the first person to move and control a single atom.

In one sense, we've been using nanotechnology for centuries: the colours in medieval stained-glass windows were the result of nanocrystals created in the heating and cooling of the glass.

WORKING AT THE NANOSCALE

For nanotechnology to work, we have to be able to manipulate atoms, not just see them.

The tiniest tweezers couldn't pick up an atom – it's just too small. So scientists have had to get creative to work with matter at this scale.

Scientists use special kinds of electron microscope, including the scanning tunnelling microscope (STM) and the atomic force microscope (AFM).

These can move atoms and molecules around like miniature building blocks using extremely sharp metal probes and tiny electric currents.

Another process is molecular beam epitaxy, which is a technique for growing single crystals very slowly, one layer of atoms at a time.

DID YOU KNOW?

In 1989, a team at the computer company IBM managed to spell out the company's initials in atoms. Using an STM electron microscope, they manipulated 35 xenon atoms to form the letters IBM.

A WORLD OF APPLICATIONS

Using nanotechnology, materials can be made stronger, lighter, more durable, more reactive and better at conducting electricity or heat.

SUPERIOR SURFACE

Nanotechnology is being used to alter the surfaces of materials to make them more resistant to dirt. Fabrics used in furnishings are coated with nanowhiskers – fibres so small that dirt can't penetrate them. Clothing fabrics can be made to resist wrinkling, staining and bacteria growth.

FACTOR 50

DID YOU KNOW?

Computers have become smaller and faster over recent years thanks to nanotechnology. By working at the nanoscale, electronic engineers can make transistors – the switches that are the basis for all computers – ever smaller.

In 2000, a typical transistor was 130 to 250 nanometres wide. By 2016, a transistor just one nanometre wide was shown at Lawrence Berkeley National Laboratory in California, USA.

MIRACLE MATERIAL

Carbon nanotubes are cylinders made of rolled-up sheets just one atom thick. Despite this, nanotubes are incredibly strong and are great conductors of heat and electricity. This could make them useful in electronics and as a material in everything from car parts to baseball bats.

DID YOU KNOW?
Carbon nanotubes might one day be used to build a lift to space, massively reducing the cost of sending up rockets.

SPACE

NANOBOTS

One day, it may be possible to build nanoscale machines with tiny wheels, gears, levers, switches, pumps and motors. Scientists have already shown how it could be done.

If you thread a molecule made of a ring of atoms through a molecule made of a rod of atoms, and if the molecules have differing electrical charges, the ring will shunt back and forth along the rod, just like a tiny piston.

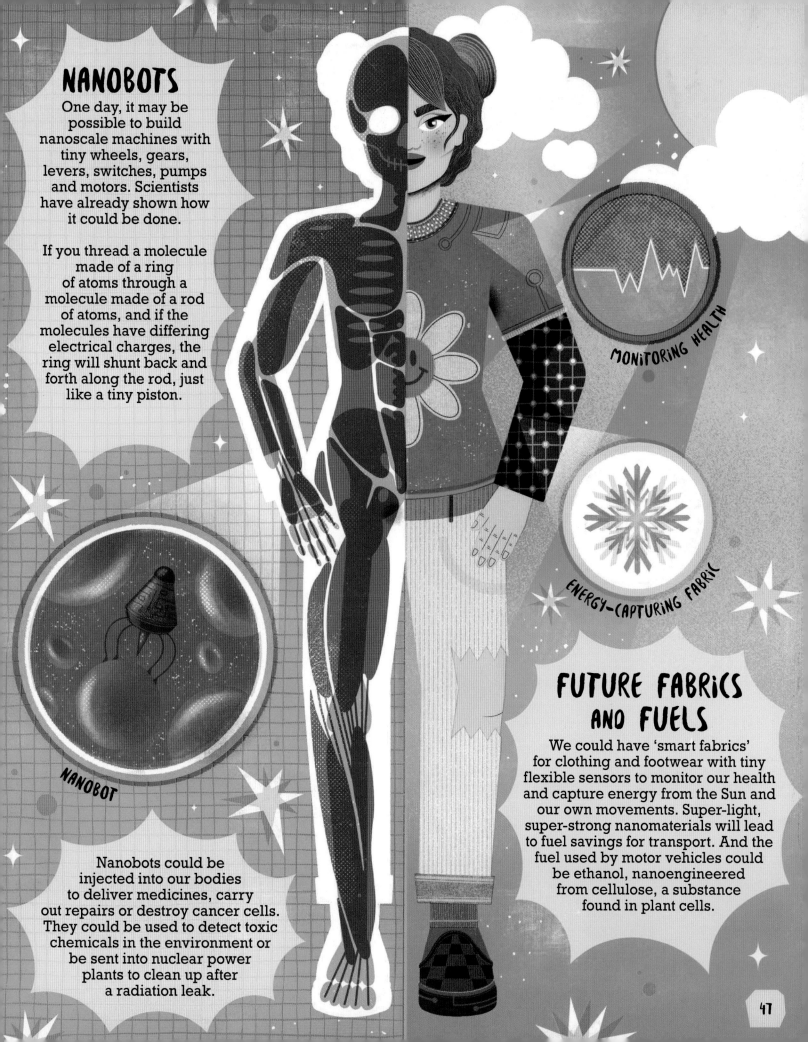

NANOBOT

MONITORING HEALTH

ENERGY-CAPTURING FABRIC

Nanobots could be injected into our bodies to deliver medicines, carry out repairs or destroy cancer cells. They could be used to detect toxic chemicals in the environment or be sent into nuclear power plants to clean up after a radiation leak.

FUTURE FABRICS AND FUELS

We could have 'smart fabrics' for clothing and footwear with tiny flexible sensors to monitor our health and capture energy from the Sun and our own movements. Super-light, super-strong nanomaterials will lead to fuel savings for transport. And the fuel used by motor vehicles could be ethanol, nanoengineered from cellulose, a substance found in plant cells.

47

MiND UPLOADiNG

Could we ever upload our minds to a computer? Perhaps the process has already begun. Today, we rely on small computers in our pockets for reminders, storing memories and accessing information. We communicate using social media.

Some have special implants to improve their hearing or vision, or to keep their hearts beating regularly. Others can move prosthetic limbs using their thoughts alone.

This gradual merging of human and machine is likely to continue. Where it will end up no one can say, but some scientists believe our ultimate destiny will be digital immortality – our minds copied and transferred onto a machine.

BODY SWAPPING

Why would we want this? We've already discussed the possibilities of physical immortality. With mind uploading, we could stop worrying about how to keep our bodies going and instead live forever in digital form.

We could even be downloaded into another, younger body when our old body gets worn out. This would avoid the problems of overpopulation caused by physical immortality.

It could allow us to go on centuries-long journeys to explore distant planets or help us survive a global environmental disaster here on Earth.

DID YOU KNOW?
In 2018, a company called Nectome offered to preserve human brains after death so that centuries later, once the technology allows it, the brains can be scanned and the data uploaded to a computer, human body or robot.

CAN IT BE DONE?

The brain is a complex organ with around 86 billion neurons (nerve cells) that are constantly connecting with one another. There are an estimated 150 trillion of these connections, and they are known as the 'connectome'. We would need to scan a living brain in great detail to map the connectome, then copy it to a computer to create an accurate simulation of a person's mind.

Scientists have already managed to map part of a rat's brain. Assuming it will become possible one day, using super-powerful computers, to map the human connectome, there's still no guarantee we'll be able to recreate a mind from that data. It could be that what we call consciousness simply cannot be recreated artificially.

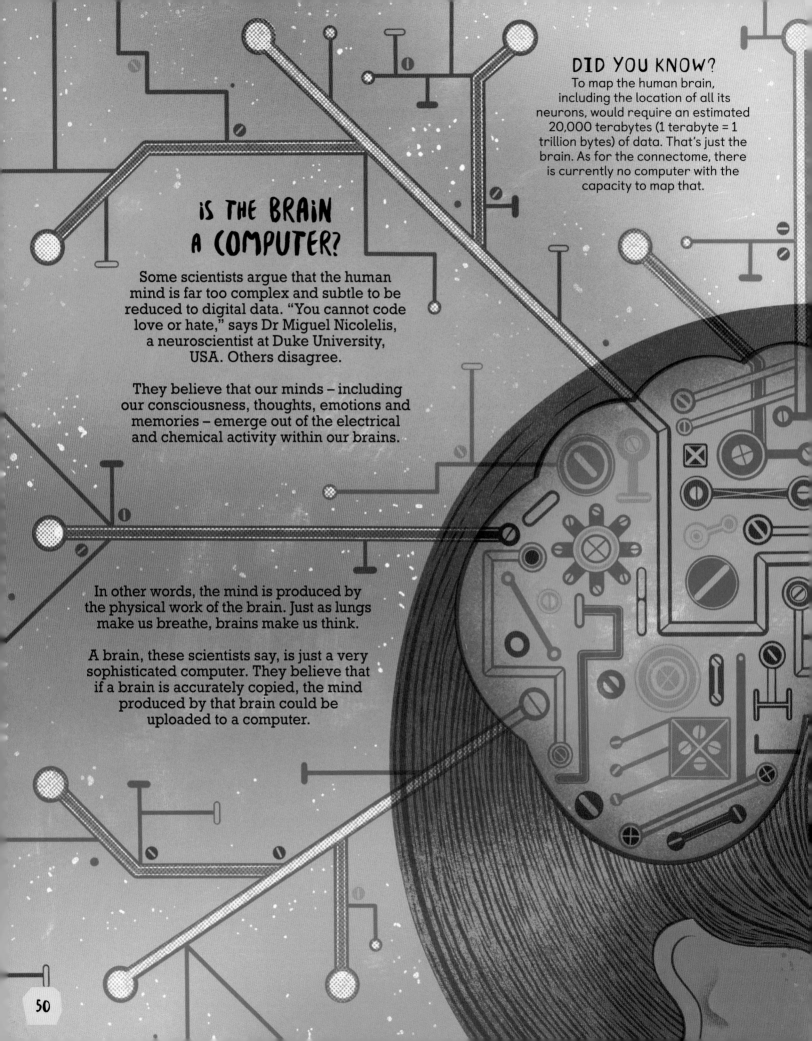

IS THE BRAIN A COMPUTER?

Some scientists argue that the human mind is far too complex and subtle to be reduced to digital data. "You cannot code love or hate," says Dr Miguel Nicolelis, a neuroscientist at Duke University, USA. Others disagree.

They believe that our minds – including our consciousness, thoughts, emotions and memories – emerge out of the electrical and chemical activity within our brains.

In other words, the mind is produced by the physical work of the brain. Just as lungs make us breathe, brains make us think.

A brain, these scientists say, is just a very sophisticated computer. They believe that if a brain is accurately copied, the mind produced by that brain could be uploaded to a computer.

DID YOU KNOW?

To map the human brain, including the location of all its neurons, would require an estimated 20,000 terabytes (1 terabyte = 1 trillion bytes) of data. That's just the brain. As for the connectome, there is currently no computer with the capacity to map that.

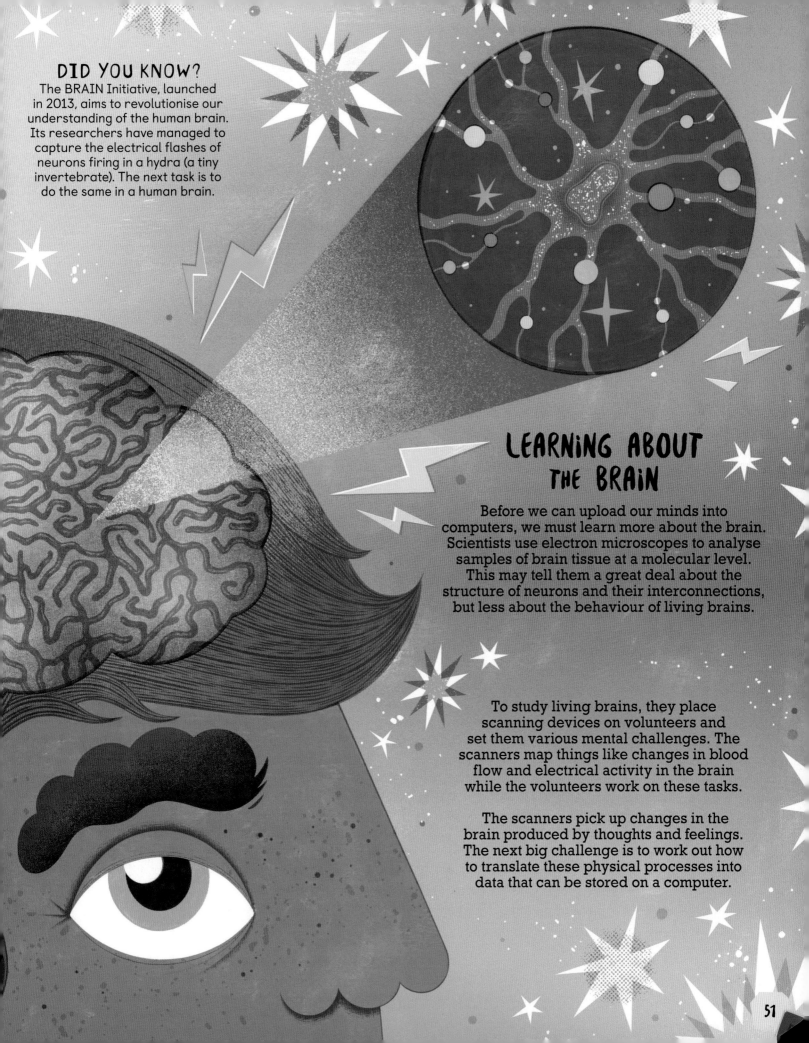

LEARNING ABOUT THE BRAIN

Before we can upload our minds into computers, we must learn more about the brain. Scientists use electron microscopes to analyse samples of brain tissue at a molecular level. This may tell them a great deal about the structure of neurons and their interconnections, but less about the behaviour of living brains.

To study living brains, they place scanning devices on volunteers and set them various mental challenges. The scanners map things like changes in blood flow and electrical activity in the brain while the volunteers work on these tasks.

The scanners pick up changes in the brain produced by thoughts and feelings. The next big challenge is to work out how to translate these physical processes into data that can be stored on a computer.

ARE MEMORIES MADE OF DATA?

The idea that memories could be encoded as data suggests that they are precise, unchanging things, but they're not. You may remember a funny incident from childhood, but this memory is unlikely to be accurate. You almost certainly amend it each time you tell the story to others.

As you get older, the memory fades and gets overlaid with different emotions. If you were to upload the memory to a computer, it would capture just one version of something that is continually evolving in your mind.

DID YOU KNOW?

Brain scientists at the University of Southern California, USA, successfully tested a 'memory implant' on rats and monkeys. A device recorded the brain's electrical activity when forming a simple short-term memory (like pushing a button to obtain food). The recording was sent to a computer, converted into a digital signal, then fed back into the brain, where it was sealed as a long-term memory.

WHICH ONE ARE YOU?

If your mind was uploaded to a computer, it would raise some tricky questions. Is the digital simulation of your mind you – or are *you* still you? The simulation might believe that your identity has been transferred to them now, along with your personality, thoughts and memories. Are you now two people?

What happens when it comes to legal matters? If the simulation commits a crime, are you liable? When you die, does the simulation inherit your property? And what if multiple copies are made of you? The technology could create some very complex situations!

A digital existence could be fun. We could download ourselves into more than one physical body to enjoy life as different people. Or, if we felt like it, we could place ourselves on a microchip and fly off into space in a tiny spaceship – or spacechip!

DO SIMULATIONS HAVE RIGHTS?

Digital people will have emotions just like physical people. They will experience joy and love as well as pain. So, if these simulations ever became a reality, they will need to be protected by laws too. Will they be allowed to marry, adopt children and vote? Or face punishment for crimes? These questions will need to be answered.

MAPPING THE MIND'S MYSTERIES

Mind uploading is a fascinating idea, but it may never be possible. The chemical reactions in our brains may not translate into data, but the research has taught us a great deal about the brain and we're going to learn a lot more in the future.

By mapping thought processes, we'll gain a greater understanding of anxiety, sleep disorders and mental illnesses; be able to create medicines to treat these conditions; and enhance our mental performance.

SUPERHUMANS

We've all seen superheroes and heroines on our screens accomplishing epic feats of strength, speed and agility. Ordinary human bystanders in these shows can only look on in slack-jawed wonder. Is it possible that one day we ordinary humans could develop superpowers of our own? Recent developments in genetic engineering and bioengineering suggest we can.

HOW WILL WE CHANGE?

Even without the added benefits of technology, our abilities as a species are improving. Thanks to better diet and nutrition, we are bigger, healthier, stronger and longer-living than our ancestors. This trend is likely to continue…

To deal with warmer temperatures and solar radiation, people's skin tones will probably become darker. Wisdom teeth, useful before we had knives, are likely to disappear. As people travel and mix, we may all become more similar-looking, too.

MACHINES IN OUR BODIES

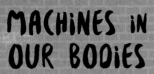

For health reasons, we place devices in our bodies, such as cochlear implants for hearing and pacemakers for our hearts. Some people are even starting to wear implants to monitor their fitness levels. Placed under the skin, they beam data about a person's health to their phone.

SKIN IMPLANTS

RADIO FREQUENCY IDENTIFICATION CHIP

DID YOU KNOW?

Some people have had tiny chips implanted in their hands. Radio Frequency Identification (RFID) chips contain personal details including an individual's medical history. In future, these could take the place of keys, credit cards and passwords. We could simply swipe our hand at doors, cars and phones to activate them and wave at a barcode to buy something.

THOUGHT CONTROL

In recent years, artificial limbs have improved dramatically. Electrodes placed in the brain, nerves and muscles enable the brain to send signals to a limb to control movement. The amputee need only imagine moving their limb, and it will move.

When a prosthetic hand touches an object, sensors send messages back to the brain, just like natural fingers. The brain can then direct the hand to manipulate the object. Eventually, prosthetic limbs will develop the dexterity and sensitivity of their natural equivalents.

DID YOU KNOW?

One day, there might be artificial organs that could replace and improve on the functions of the heart, liver and kidneys. These devices would not be vulnerable to disease, and they would pump the blood and remove toxins more efficiently than natural organs.

In addition, we could have fleets of nanobots sailing through our bloodstream, zapping germs and repairing injuries. We would, in effect, become cyborgs – part human, part machine.

SUPER SENSES

In the future, we'll start making changes to our bodies not just to stay healthy but to improve our abilities. Imagine changing your eyesight so you can see hundreds of new colours or see in the dark. This may become possible with retinal implants containing graphene.

In normal hearing, sound waves strike our eardrums. These vibrate against three tiny ear bones, which then push against a fluid-filled structure called the cochlea. The cochlea translates the pressure waves into nerve signals that are interpreted in the brain as sounds.

Some deaf people use a 'bone conduction' device that enables sound waves to bypass the eardrums and vibrate the ear bones directly. Scientists are currently exploring bone conduction as a means of expanding our range so we can hear ultrasonic vibrations.

BONE CONDUCTION DEVICE

SEISMIC ACTIVITY SENSOR

People may even design their own senses. In earthquake-prone regions, you might install sensors in your feet to detect seismic activity, warning of an impending quake.

If you have a poor sense of direction, why not implant an inner compass in your eye, like those of migratory birds?

Or you could adapt your ears to perceive atmospheric pressure, allowing you to predict the weather.

BRAIN CONTROL

Today, there are 'smart drugs' available called nootropics, designed to improve mental ability.

Neural implants can also be placed in the brain to treat people with injuries and disabilities. They consist of tiny electrodes that communicate with the body's healthy neurons in order to stimulate damaged parts of the nervous system.

They allow amputees to move artificial limbs or help paralysed patients regain control of their bodies. In future, they may be used by anyone to enhance memory, physical movement and the senses. They could allow us to control devices such as computers or cars. Imagine directing a drone with your thoughts!

DID YOU KNOW?
The colour-blind Irish-born artist Neil Harbisson has had an antenna implanted in his skull that allows him to 'hear' colours.

It detects the wavelength of the colours he sees and translates them into musical notes.

French-Israeli neuroscientist Moran Cerf and his team placed electrodes inside the brains of patients undergoing surgery. The electrodes created detours, enabling patients to access different parts of their brain at will. For example, they could see a beautiful scene in their minds even while looking at an ugly one or choose to ignore the mean words of a bully. This could be used to treat people with depression.

HIVE MIND

Neural implants could even allow us to connect to the internet and access the combined knowledge of everyone on the planet. This could be the first step towards a 'hive mind' (a single collective human consciousness).

Some believe this could threaten our individuality. Imagine the hive mind being exploited by corporations eager to sell us things or politicians wishing to control us.

ALTERING OUR GENES

We inherit many diseases from our parents through our genes, and these can be treated through genetic engineering. A revolutionary new gene-editing tool, called CRISPR, allows scientists to target a particular DNA sequence, remove the genes that cause a disease and replace them with new, healthy genes.

Scientists might one day use CRISPR to boost almost any desired human trait. Governments may develop superhuman soldiers with genes altered for physical and mental strength, courage, stamina, intelligence, pain resistance and less need for sleep. But scientists have so far struggled to find the genes responsible for qualities such as intelligence, so a lot more research will be needed.

DID YOU KNOW?

CRISPR was discovered by Emmanuelle Charpentier and Jennifer Doudna in 2012. While researching how bacteria fight viral infections, they discovered a protein, Cas9, which is able to seek out, cut and degrade a virus's DNA. They found that it was possible to harness Cas9's ability to delete or insert pieces of DNA with absolute precision.

DESIGNER BABIES

Another process, called 'germline engineering', involves the editing of genes in sperm, eggs or embryos, usually in order to eliminate genes that cause disease.

But this affects future generations, as yet unborn, who have no say over the procedure. It has the potential to create 'designer babies' – children with traits chosen by their parents. For these reasons, germline engineering on humans is banned in more than 40 countries.

HE JIANKUI

DID YOU KNOW?

In 2018, Chinese scientist He Jiankui revealed he had used CRISPR to create the world's first genetically edited babies – twin girls Lulu and Nana. He used the gene-editing tool to remove a gene called CCR5, which can cause the disease HIV, hoping this would make the babies resistant to the disease.

This experiment was widely criticised by the scientific community. Some warn that removing this gene could make the girls and their future offspring vulnerable to other diseases.

SHOULD WE BECOME 'GODS'?

There may be dangers in this desire to turn ourselves into superhumans since any mistakes made may affect future generations.

These powers could be exploited. For example, a regime protected by an army of genetically enhanced super-soldiers could decide to turn them against their own citizens to keep itself in power.

Imagine a future where these technologies are available, but only for the rich. This could mean a division in society.

Famine and war could follow as the elite take control of Earth's resources and the masses resist. So, we must proceed very carefully. Some technologies might have to be banned altogether – others should be made available to all.

We may eventually see that the best superpower of all is the one we were born with: the power to think, learn and imagine. With our imperfect biological brains and bodies, we've already solved many of the mysteries of the universe.

Of course, we could always go further and turn ourselves into genetically modified cyborgs. But in doing so, might we not risk losing our humanity?